Art and Civilization

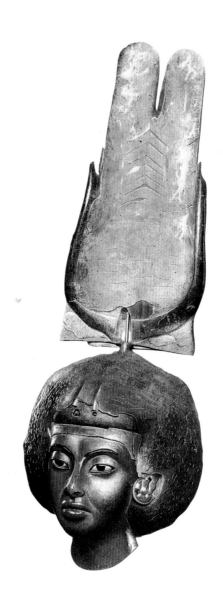

*Other titles in the series
Art and Civilization:*

Prehistory
Ancient Greece
Ancient Rome
The Medieval World
The Renaissance

Ancient Egypt

Neil Morris

Illustrations by Paola Ravaglia, Alessandro Cantucci,
Fabiano Fabbrucci, Andrea Morandi, Matteo Chesi

PETER BEDRICK BOOKS

NEW YORK

Published in the United States in 2000
by PETER BEDRICK BOOKS
A division of NTC/Contemporary Publishing Group, Inc.
4255 West Touhy Avenue, Lincolnwood (Chicago), Illinois
60646-1975 U.S.A.
Library of Congress Cataloging-in-Publication CIP data
is available from the United States Library of Congress

The Renaissance was created and produced by
McRae Books Srl, via de' Rustici, 5 – Florence (Italy)
e-mail: mcrae@tin.it

Text: Neil Morris
Main illustrations Paola Ravaglia, Studio Stalio (Alessandro Cantucci,
Fabiano Fabbrucci, Andrea Morandi), Matteo Chesi
Other illustrations: Gian paolo Faleschini
Picture research: Anne McRae
Graphic Design: Marco Nardi, Anne McRae
Editing: Ronne Randall
Layout and cutouts: Ornella Fassio, Adriano Nardi
Color separations Fotolito Toscana, Florence and Litocolor, Florence

Printed in Italy by Giunti Industrie Grafiche, Prato
International Standard Book Number: 0-87226-617-6

01 02 03 15 14 13 12 11 10 9 8 7 6 5 4 3 2

Contents

Introduction

Ancient Egyptian civilization began around 3100 BC when the king of Upper Egypt, probably a man called Narmer, conquered the Delta area (known as Lower Egypt) and united the Two Lands. It was one of the earliest civilizations in the world and also one of the most long-lasting, flourishing for around 3,000 years. By the time Ancient Greece reached its zenith in 450 BC, Egyptian civilization was already more than 2,500 years old! ancient Egypt was a long, narrow country stretching along the banks of the River Nile until it reached the Delta, where it broadened as the river fanned out into many tributaries. Each year the Nile flooded the flats next to the river, covering them with fertile silt. When the floodwaters withdrew, farmers planted their crops and harvested enough food to sustain a magnificent civilization.

This tiny ivory statue shows a 1st dynasty king wearing a decorated cloak. It dates from around 2900 BC.

1.   **2.**   **3.**

After Egypt was united the White Crown (1) of Upper Egypt was combined with the Red Crown (2) of Lower Egypt to form the Double Crown(3) worn by all pharaohs for 3,000 years.

Predynastic times

Humans have been living in the Nile Valley for at least 700,000 years. However, most traces of early humans have been buried or washed away by the yearly floods. The record becomes clearer from around 4500 BC and this period, which lasted until Egypt was united under the first pharaoh, is called "Predynastic." Predynastic Egyptians lived in complex farming societies with kings, priests and rich and poor people. They produced beautiful pottery and skillfully made artifacts, like the vase and ivory-handled knife shown here.

This detail from a pharaoh's crown shows the vulture symbol of Upper Egypt and the cobra symbol of Lower Egypt. These same symbols were used throughout ancient Egyptian times. This one was made in the 18th dynasty during New Kingdom times.

LOWER EGYPT

• Avaris

• Heliopolis

Giza •

Memphis •

FAYUM

River Nile

RED SEA

WESTERN DESERT

EASTERN DESERT

• Amarna

UPPER EGYPT

Abydos •

Thebes / Luxor •

Hierakonpolis •

Elephantin

The Narmer Palette (Side A)

Found in 1898 at Hierakonpolis, the Narmer Palette is dedicated by King Narmer, who is thought to be the same person as Menes, the legendary first king of united Egypt. On one side it shows Narmer (1), wearing the White Crown (2) of Upper Egypt, in the act of hitting a prisoner over the head with a mace (3) while the falcon god, Horus (4), looks on. The meaning of the scene is made clear by Horus, the god of kingship, grabbing hold of a papyrus plant with his claw (5) to show that he now controls the Delta (Lower Egypt).

The river of life

Egypt is sometimes called "the gift of the Nile" because without its life-giving waters the country would be a barren desert. The river is formed of three tributaries – the White Nile, the Atbara and the Blue Nile – which rise far to the south, in East Africa. It is the longest river in the world and flows for 3,400 miles before it reaches the Nile Valley. It runs 650 miles through the Valley, then another 100 miles in the broad Delta plain before draining into the Mediterranean Sea in the north.

The Narmer Palette (Side B)

On the other side of the palette, King Narmer (1) is wearing the Red Crown (2) of Lower Egypt as he marches in a procession of high officials (3) to inspect two rows of beheaded enemies. Below them are two lions (4) with very long entwined necks. Their necks frame a small disk used to grind cosmetics (5). The lions are symbols of the king's control over powerful opposing forces and show that he maintains balance in Egyptian society. At the bottom of the palette the king is shown as a raging bull (6) trampling town walls and goring people. This signifies the power the king could use to maintain balance.

The Egyptian year

The Egyptian calendar was based on the cycle of the Nile. The year was divided into three seasons of four months each. The first, called *akhet*, began when the floodwaters rose, and lasted from July to October. Farmers could not work the land during this time and were employed by the state on building projects. When the floodwaters receded *peret* began. Lasting from November to February, this was the season when farmers plowed the silt-covered fields and sowed the new crops. The final season, *shemu*, was the busiest in the year: intense labor was required to reap, thresh, winnow and store the grain and harvest all the other crops.

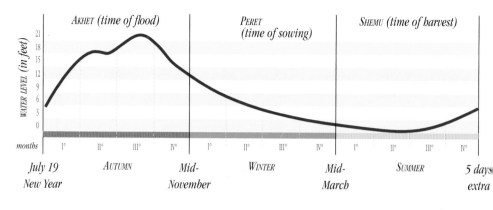

	AKHET (time of flood)	PERET (time of sowing)	SHEMU (time of harvest)

The Egyptian year was divided into three four month seasons. This was the model for our own twelve-month calendar.

Farmin

The vast majority of ancient Egyptians worked
farmers or farm laborers. The main crops grow
were barley and emmer, which were used to make the stap
food and drink – bread and beer. The ground wa
prepared using a simple ox-drawn plow or by han
with hoes. The seed was scattered by hand. A
harvest time wooden sickles with flint tee
were used to cut the grain, and donkeys carried
back to the threshing floor. Wealthy farmers owne
cattle and oxen which they kept for meat or used
plow the fields. Sheep and goats were also kept fo
their milk, meat and woo

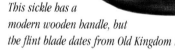

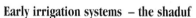

Early irrigation systems – the shaduf

The Egyptians built canals out from the River Nile to obtain water for irrigation. The shaduf (shown in the wall painting above), a bucket on a rope attached to an upright post weighted with a stone or lump of mud, was used to lift water from the river or canals to water gardens during the dry season.

This sickle has a modern wooden handle, but the flint blade dates from Old Kingdom times.

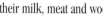

This wall painting from Thebes shows two men harvesting grapes.

Winemaking

The Egyptians made and drank both red and white wine. After harvesting, the grapes were trodden to release the juice, which was left to ferment in large earthenware jars. After several months, or even years, it was flavored with honey and spices or sweetened with dates. Wine was also made from dates, figs and pomegranates.

This wall painting shows farm workers winnowing the grain from the chaff in the open air. The same method is still used in many parts of Egypt today.

Model of cattle being counted for tax purposes

This model comes from a tomb. The tomb owner is shown sitting in a chair in the center of the raised platform (1). He is surrounded by scribes

and officials (2) who are counting the cattle being driven before them by herdsmen (3). The cattle, of many different colors, are controlled by ropes attached to their horns (4) or by halters (5). In front of the platform a man is being punished by flogging (6), for some wrongdoing which we will never know.

The Pyramid Builders

During the early dynastic period Egypt was fragmented by local disputes and almost in a state of civil war. However, when the 3rd dynasty king Djoser came to power he established a strong, well-governed society with its capital at Memphis. Djoser's reign ushered in a period of stability and great wealth known as the Old Kingdom (c. 2686–2125 BC). During this time the concept of kingship changed and the kings came to be seen as gods. In keeping with their immense wealth and power, they began to build huge pyramid-shaped tombs. Many of the pyramids have survived to the present day and they are among the most striking remains of ancient Egyptian civilization.

This beautiful bird's head in gold represents Horus, the protector god of kings. It was made during Old Kingdom times.

Imhotep (left) was one of Djoser's most loyal and able advisors. He was revered by the ancient Egyptians for thousands of years as an architect, mathematician, astronomer, writer and doctor. Imhotep designed and built the first Step Pyramid.

Snefru (c. 2613–2589 BC) was the greatest pyramid builder in Egyptian history. He was the first king to build true geometric pyramids rather than the earlier step pyramids. During his life he built three full-sized pyramids and two smaller ones. Archaeologists have calculated that he was responsible for moving some 27 million cubic feet of stone!

The step pyramid

During the early dynastic period the kings of Egypt were buried in flat-topped mastaba tombs built of mud bricks. Djoser's Step Pyramid was the first large scale monument in the world to be built entirely of stone. It was a huge step forward in terms of technical and artistic progress. The pyramid is surrounded by many buildings, including the North and South Pavilions, large temples and terraces, carved façades, columns, platforms, shrines, chapels and life-sized statues. The enclosure wall contains an area of 37 acres, about the same size as a large town of those times.

Djoser's Step Pyramid at Saqqara w the first of Egypt's pyramids. But entirely in stone, it is remarkable monument the architectur abilities of th ancien Egyptian

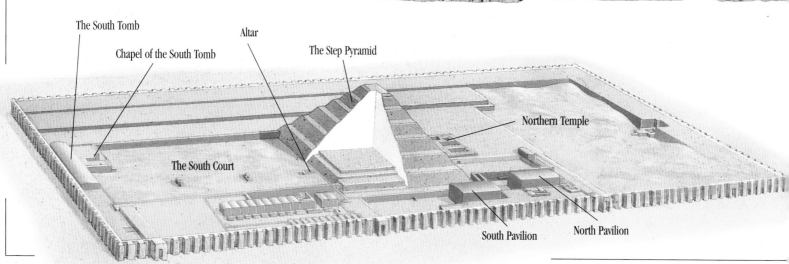

The South Tomb

Chapel of the South Tomb

Altar

The Step Pyramid

The South Court

Northern Temple

South Pavilion

North Pavilion

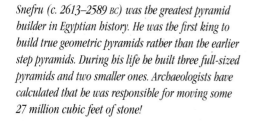

The pyramids at Giza

Pyramid building reached its peak at Giza. The pyramids there, built over the span of three generations, by Cheops, his son Chephren, and Mycerinus, are large and well-constructed. Although built last, Mycerinus's pyramid (1) is the smallest of the three. The three small pyramids in front of it (2) were built as tombs for Mycerinus's queens. Chephren's pyramid, in the center, (3), dominates the plain, although it is actually slightly smaller than Cheops's Great Pyramid (4) which was built at a lower level. The Great Sphinx (right) is attached to Chephren's complex.

The man-headed lion statue of the Sphinx crouches at the foot of Chephren's causeway. It was cut from a natural outcrop of rock and stands almost 65 feet high and 240 feet long.

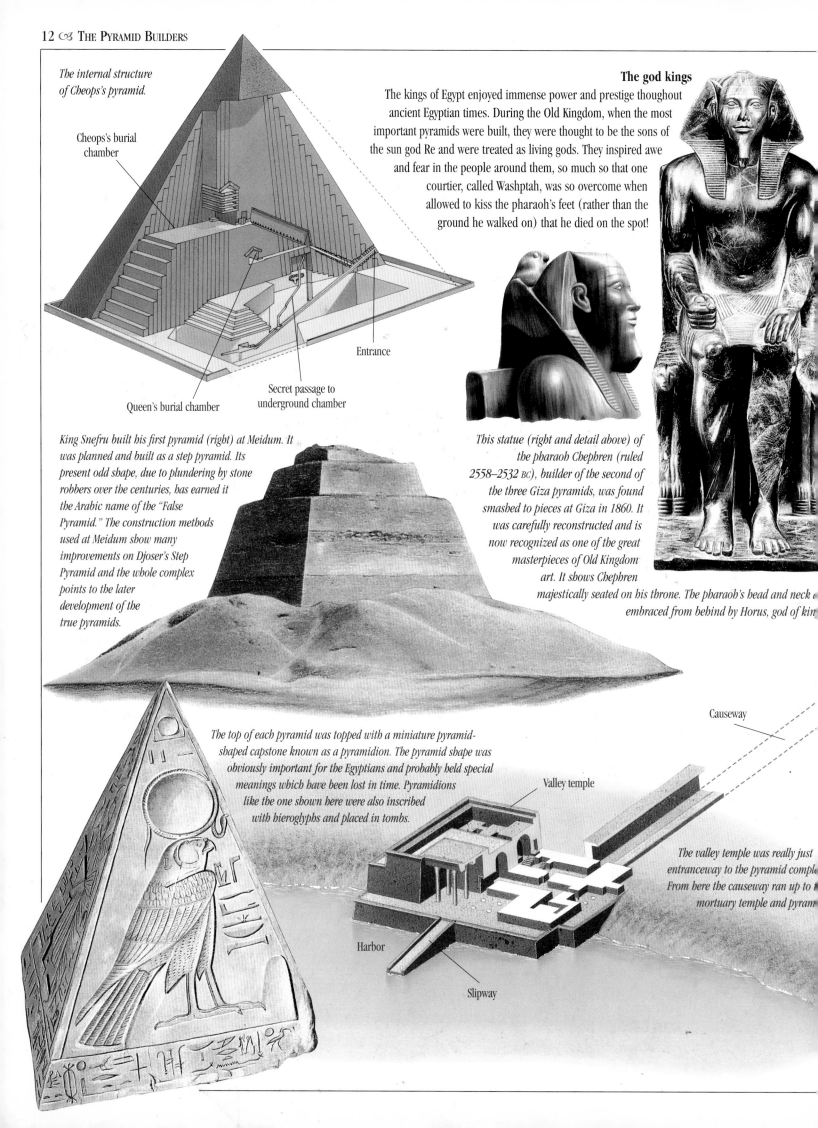

The internal structure of Cheops's pyramid.

Cheops's burial chamber

Queen's burial chamber

Secret passage to underground chamber

Entrance

The god kings

The kings of Egypt enjoyed immense power and prestige thoughout ancient Egyptian times. During the Old Kingdom, when the most important pyramids were built, they were thought to be the sons of the sun god Re and were treated as living gods. They inspired awe and fear in the people around them, so much so that one courtier, called Washptah, was so overcome when allowed to kiss the pharaoh's feet (rather than the ground he walked on) that he died on the spot!

King Snefru built his first pyramid (right) at Meidum. It was planned and built as a step pyramid. Its present odd shape, due to plundering by stone robbers over the centuries, has earned it the Arabic name of the "False Pyramid." The construction methods used at Meidum show many improvements on Djoser's Step Pyramid and the whole complex points to the later development of the true pyramids.

This statue (right and detail above) of the pharaoh Chephren (ruled 2558–2532 BC), builder of the second of the three Giza pyramids, was found smashed to pieces at Giza in 1860. It was carefully reconstructed and is now recognized as one of the great masterpieces of Old Kingdom art. It shows Chephren majestically seated on his throne. The pharaoh's head and neck embraced from behind by Horus, god of kin

Causeway

The top of each pyramid was topped with a miniature pyramid-shaped capstone known as a pyramidion. The pyramid shape was obviously important for the Egyptians and probably held special meanings which have been lost in time. Pyramidions like the one shown here were also inscribed with hieroglyphs and placed in tombs.

Valley temple

The valley temple was really just entranceway to the pyramid comple From here the causeway ran up to mortuary temple and pyram

Harbor

Slipway

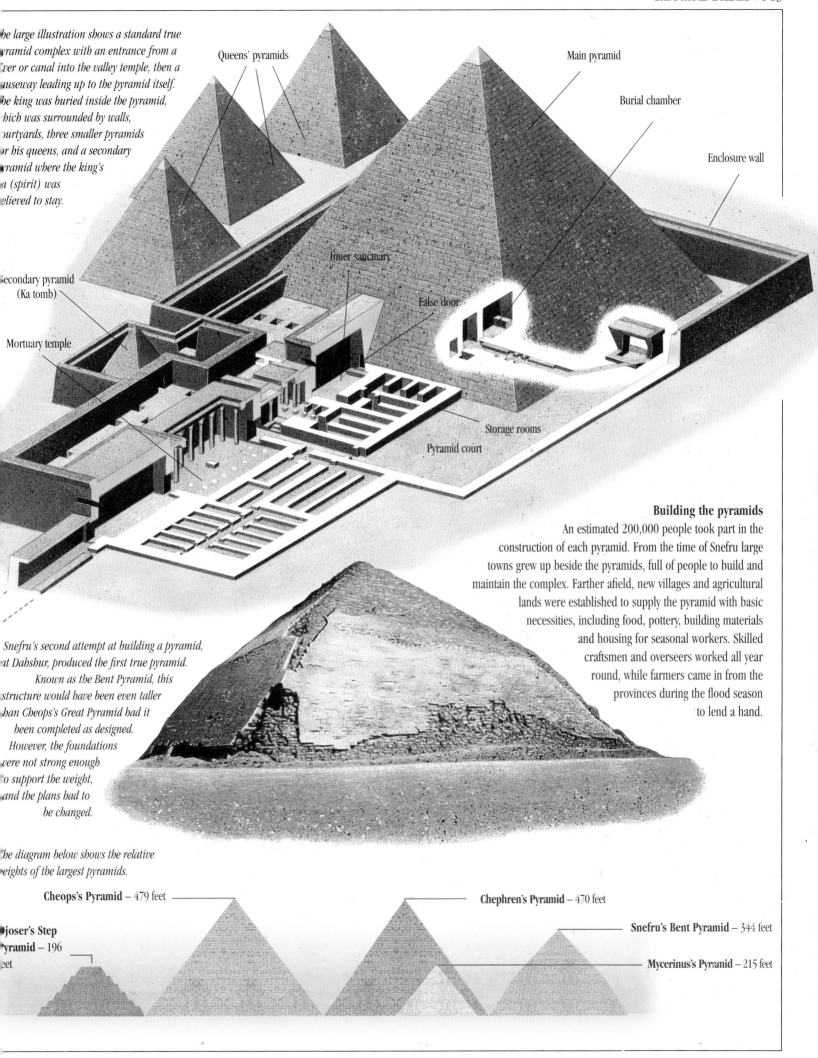

...he large illustration shows a standard true
...yramid complex with an entrance from a
...ver or canal into the valley temple, then a
...auseway leading up to the pyramid itself.
...he king was buried inside the pyramid,
...hich was surrounded by walls,
...ourtyards, three smaller pyramids
...or his queens, and a secondary
...yramid where the king's
...a (spirit) was
...elieved to stay.

Queens' pyramids

Main pyramid

Burial chamber

Enclosure wall

...econdary pyramid
(Ka tomb)

Inner sanctuary

False door

Mortuary temple

Storage rooms

Pyramid court

Building the pyramids
An estimated 200,000 people took part in the
construction of each pyramid. From the time of Snefru large
towns grew up beside the pyramids, full of people to build and
maintain the complex. Farther afield, new villages and agricultural
lands were established to supply the pyramid with basic
necessities, including food, pottery, building materials
and housing for seasonal workers. Skilled
craftsmen and overseers worked all year
round, while farmers came in from the
provinces during the flood season
to lend a hand.

Snefru's second attempt at building a pyramid,
...t Dahshur, produced the first true pyramid.
Known as the Bent Pyramid, this
structure would have been even taller
...han Cheops's Great Pyramid had it
been completed as designed.
However, the foundations
...ere not strong enough
...o support the weight,
...and the plans had to
be changed.

...he diagram below shows the relative
...eights of the largest pyramids.

Cheops's Pyramid – 479 feet

Chephren's Pyramid – 470 feet

...joser's Step
...yramid – 196
...eet

Snefru's Bent Pyramid – 344 feet

Mycerinus's Pyramid – 215 feet

Gods and Goddesses

There were many gods and goddesses in ancient Egypt. Some, such as Osiris, Isis, Horus, Hathor, Anubis and Thoth were recognized throughout Egypt, while others were local gods whose names would not even be known in a neighboring village even a short distance away. The roles of many deities evolved over the centuries; sometimes two gods combined, as in the case of Amun and Ra, who became the potent creator god Amun-Ra. Local gods often became national gods when someone from their village became powerful in central government, elevating his own gods to power too. The pharaoh's local gods were usually the most powerful at any given time.

The wall painting below comes from Pharaoh Horemheb's tomb in the Valley of the Kings. Horemheb became king unexpectedly. He was a high-ranking military officer when the young Pharaoh Tutankhamun died in 1325 BC leaving no heirs. Tutankhamun was succeeded by Ay, who married his widow. However, Ay was old when he took the throne and only ruled for four years. Horemheb ruled for 28 years. He died leaving two tombs: a modest one in Saqqara, built in his youth when he had no idea that he would become king; and another very splendid one in the Valley of the Kings, built after he became pharaoh.

Wall painting in the tomb of Pharaoh Horemheb

The painting shows the pharaoh standing before various gods and goddesses. Wearing a loincloth and a royal headdress, Horemheb (2) offers cups of wine to Osiris (1), one of the most important Egyptian gods. As Lord of the Underworld, Osiris gave life through the Nile flood and the crops it brought each year. He was also identified with the pharaohs when they died, who became gods themselves. In the next scene Horemheb (4) stands before the goddess Hathor (3), the most widely worshiped goddess in Egypt. Hathor was a symbol of strength and fury but also of sweet motherly and womanly love. In the next scene Horemheb (6) offers wine to Horus (5), the god of kings. Originally a god of Lower Egypt, Horus became known as the son of Osiris and Isis and the protector of pharaohs. He was usually shown as a falcon or as a man with a falcon's head. The goddess on the far right is Isis (7), one of the most important goddesses in Egypt.

The gods and goddesses of creation

According to a well-known creation myth Amun-Ra, the creator, rose from the watery depths of Nun wrapped in the petals of a lotus flower. He then created his son Shu, the god of air, and his daughter Tefnut, goddess of the dew and moisture. Shu and Tefnut had a son, Geb, the earth god, and a daughter Nut, the sky goddess. In their turn, Geb and Nut had four children – Osiris, Seth, Isis and Nephthys – who lived on earth.

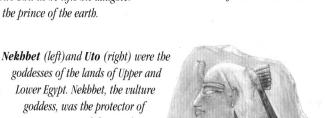

*This painting from a mummy case shows **Shu** as he lifts his daughter **Nut**, the sky goddess, away from **Geb**, the prince of the earth.*

The importance of order

Maintaining Maat, or correct world order, was the main object in the practice of ancient Egyptian religion. Egyptians believed that the world was born of disorder and that it would ultimately return to disorder. Their task was to defend life and order from the agents of chaos and disorder.

Maat, the goddess of truth, justice and orderly conduct, was shown as a kneeling woman with an ostrich feather in her hair.

***Amun-Ra** was shown with the attributes of kingship – a tall gold crown, the kingly beard and the scepter.*

***Amun-Ra**, who was revered as the creator and king of the gods, was a composite of two earlier gods, Amun and Ra. Amun was a local god in southern Egypt. When his cult spread to Thebes he became the god of the pharaohs. At about the same time he became associated with Ra, the sun god of Heliopolis.*

***Nekhbet** (left) and **Uto** (right) were the goddesses of the lands of Upper and Lower Egypt. Nekhbet, the vulture goddess, was the protector of Upper Egypt, while Uto, the serpent goddess was the protector of Lower Egypt. When Egypt was united the kings wore a crown with both the vulture and the serpent on the front.*

***Sekhmet**, "the mighty one", was a fierce goddess of war and defender of the creator god Ptah, who was also her husband. She was usually shown as a lioness or a woman with a lion's head topped with a sun disk with a snake at the front.*

*The ancient **Thoth** was the god of knowledge and of scribes. He was shown either as a baboon or an ibis. Thoth became associated with the dead because he recorded Anubis's decision regarding the dead person's soul during the weighing of the heart ceremony (see page 21).*

***Ptah** was originally the local god of Memphis, the Old Kingdom capital of Egypt. He was a powerful creator god who called things on earth into being by naming them. He was the patron god of craftspeople, especially of sculptors. Ptah was always shown as a man with a mummified body, wearing a blue skullcap and holding a scepter of power.*

*Sanctuaries to the crocodile god **Sobek** were located along the Nile in places where crocodiles posed the greatest threats to humans.*

Seth was usually shown with a curved, pointed snout, square-tipped ears and slanting eyes. Originally a sky god from Upper Egypt and later the brother of Osiris, he was always a troublesome god who brought disorder and chaos. In a famous myth he kills his brother Osiris and fights against Osiris's son Horus for control of Egypt.

The goddess Nephthys was Isis's sister and often helped her in her endeavors. Wife of Seth, she was also a protector of the dead.

Isis was one of the most important goddesses of ancient Egypt. In a well-known myth, she put the pieces of her husband Osiris's body back together after he was killed by Seth. She then gave birth to Horus, god of kings. She had very strong powers and could heal the sick and bring the dead back to life. As the mother of Horus, she was worshiped as a mother and fertility goddess. She was shown as a woman with the hieroglyphic sign for "throne" on her head.

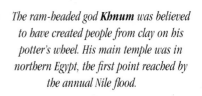

The ram-headed god **Khnum** was believed to have created people from clay on his potter's wheel. His main temple was in northern Egypt, the first point reached by the annual Nile flood.

Anubis, lord and protector of the dead in Old Kingdom times, was responsible for preparing the bodies of the dead for the afterlife. He was said to be the inventor of the embalming technique. Later, he also became the conductor of souls to the afterlife. He was shown as a man with a jackal's head.

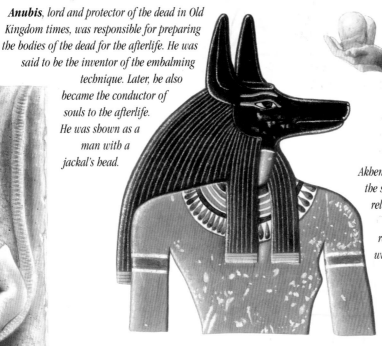

Akhenaten makes an offering to the sun. According to the new religion Akhenaten was the only way people could reach the afterlife. Osiris was dropped and images of Nefertiti, Akhenaten's queen, replaced those of all the other goddesses.

The dwarf god **Bes** was associated with gaiety, feasting, children and childbirth. With his squat body, bow legs, protruding tongue and goggle eyes he was quite ugly, perhaps to scare off evil spirits. Usually shown full-faced rather than in profile, Bes was different in appearance from the other gods and was probably adopted from Africa or Arabia.

Akhenaten (Amenhotep IV) 1350–1334 BC

During the 18th dynasty, the pharaoh Amenhotep IV radically changed Egyptian religion. Early in his reign Amenhotep changed his name to Akhenaten, meaning "of service to Aten (the sun)." Unlike all the other Egyptian pharaohs before and after him, Akhenaten worshiped only one god – Aten. All other gods and goddesses, including household deities, were excluded. Akhenaten dedicated a long poem to Aten (which is quite similar to Psalm 104 in the Biblical tradition): "Thou arisest fair in the horizon of Heaven, O Living Aten, Beginner of Life... there is none who knows thee save thy son Akhenaten." The new religion made it clear that people could only contact God through Akhenaten. He outlawed the priesthood (which had became more and more powerful over the centuries) and closed the temples. He also moved the capital to a new site called Akhetaten (later el-Amarna) where he built a city dedicated to Aten. After his death Akhetaten was abandoned and Egypt returned to the old gods and goddesses.

Inside a sarcophagus

The mummified bodies of some kings, such as Tutankhamun (ruled 1336–1327 BC), were put inside an elaborate set of coffins. These were to show royal status, to help protect the mummy even more, and to prevent robbery or interference by anyone who got inside the tomb. The king's body was first mummified, and then wrapped in linen with jewels, weapons and other objects. A gold mask was put over the face, and the mummy was placed in a tight-fitting coffin made of beaten gold. This was placed inside another coffin, which was made of gilded wood inlaid with colored glass, with a linen pall and more valuable objects. This was sometimes put inside a third coffin, and then the closed group of nested coffins were lowered into a stone sarcophagus. Tutankhamun's sarcophagus was found inside four rectangular, gilded wooden shrines. Fortunately, when they were discovered in 1923, tomb robbers had not gotten beyond the first shrine.

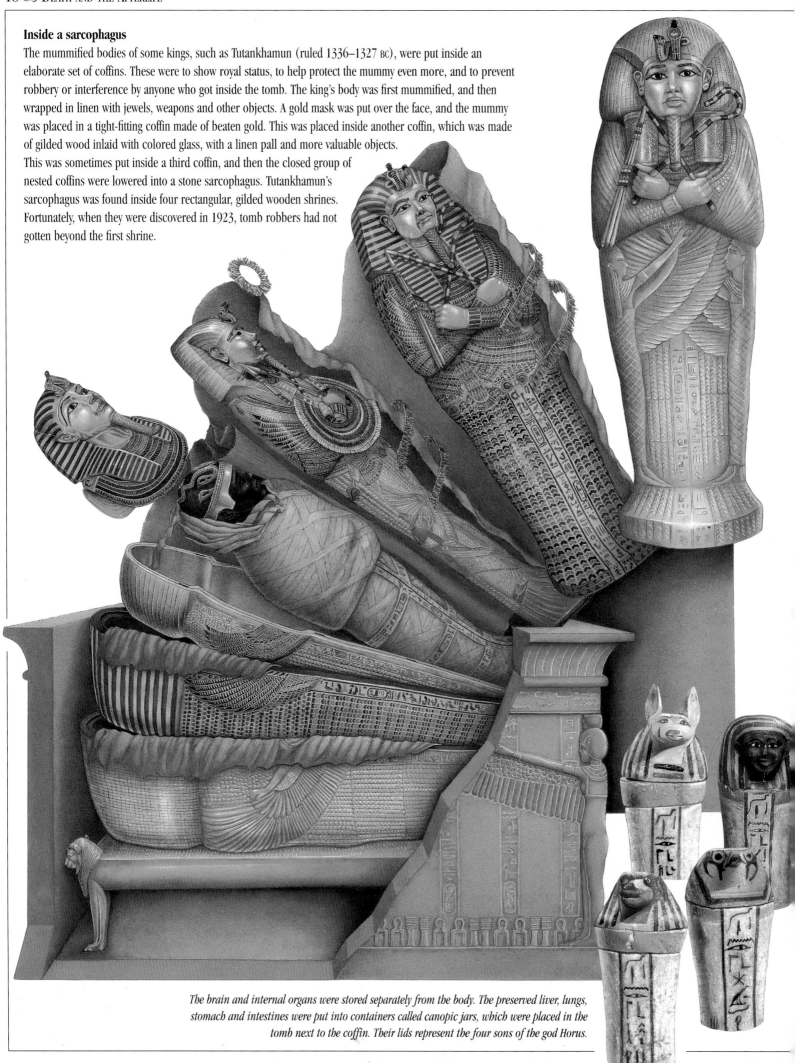

The brain and internal organs were stored separately from the body. The preserved liver, lungs, stomach and intestines were put into containers called canopic jars, which were placed in the tomb next to the coffin. Their lids represent the four sons of the god Horus.

Death and the Afterlife

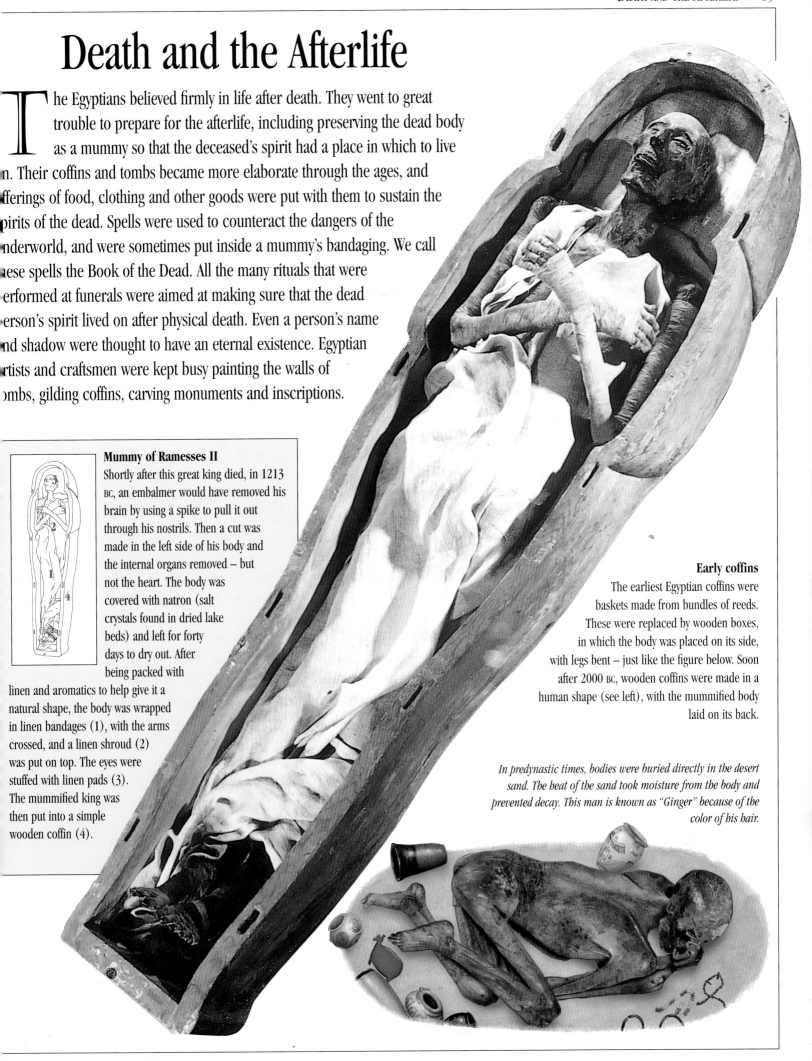

The Egyptians believed firmly in life after death. They went to great trouble to prepare for the afterlife, including preserving the dead body as a mummy so that the deceased's spirit had a place in which to live in. Their coffins and tombs became more elaborate through the ages, and offerings of food, clothing and other goods were put with them to sustain the spirits of the dead. Spells were used to counteract the dangers of the underworld, and were sometimes put inside a mummy's bandaging. We call these spells the Book of the Dead. All the many rituals that were performed at funerals were aimed at making sure that the dead person's spirit lived on after physical death. Even a person's name and shadow were thought to have an eternal existence. Egyptian artists and craftsmen were kept busy painting the walls of tombs, gilding coffins, carving monuments and inscriptions.

Mummy of Ramesses II

Shortly after this great king died, in 1213 BC, an embalmer would have removed his brain by using a spike to pull it out through his nostrils. Then a cut was made in the left side of his body and the internal organs removed – but not the heart. The body was covered with natron (salt crystals found in dried lake beds) and left for forty days to dry out. After being packed with linen and aromatics to help give it a natural shape, the body was wrapped in linen bandages (1), with the arms crossed, and a linen shroud (2) was put on top. The eyes were stuffed with linen pads (3). The mummified king was then put into a simple wooden coffin (4).

Early coffins

The earliest Egyptian coffins were baskets made from bundles of reeds. These were replaced by wooden boxes, in which the body was placed on its side, with legs bent – just like the figure below. Soon after 2000 BC, wooden coffins were made in a human shape (see left), with the mummified body laid on its back.

In predynastic times, bodies were buried directly in the desert sand. The heat of the sand took moisture from the body and prevented decay. This man is known as "Ginger" because of the color of his hair.

Wall painting of the afterlife

This wall painting, dating from about 1280 BC, was found in the burial chamber of an overseer of a village. Sennedjem (1), the overseer, and his wife Iyneferty (2), are shown in the afterlife in a field of reeds called Iaru. This is surrounded by life-giving water (3) and is the Egyptian form of heaven, or paradise. There people can enjoy doing all the things they did in life, for eternity. The couple pull up flax (4), sow and plow (5), and cut and harvest grain (6). The falcon-headed sun god Ra-Horakhty (7), combining Ra and Horus, sails through the underworld, praised by two baboons (8).

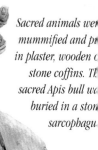

Sacred animals were mummified and p[...] in plaster, wooden [...] stone coffins. Th[...] sacred Apis bull wa[...] buried in a ston[...] sarcophagu[...]

This model of servants was placed in a tomb to help do the dead person's work in the afterlife. Food was also offered, as well as clothing, cosmetics and jewelry.

Funeral boat

Small model boats were often placed in tombs. These were meant to help the dead on their voyage through the underworld. In this wooden model from around 1900 BC, the mummy is watched over by two female mourners representing the goddesses Isis and Nephthys. The boat is steered by a sailor with two large steering oars.

Anubis was the jackal-headed god of the dead, and he was thought to be in charge of the ritual of embalming. This tomb painting shows the god preparing a mummy. In real life, the chief priest wore an Anubis mask during mummification.

Anubis holds a mummy upright as a ceremony is performed. A priest touches the mummy's mouth with a special instrument. This was thought to bring life back to the body so that the dead person could eat and speak. Another priest, wearing a leopard skin, spreads incense.

Egyptians believed they needed their heart after death, which is why it was not removed from the body. They thought that their heart was weighed against the feather of Maat, the ibis-headed goddess of truth. Anubis helped tip the balance in favor of the heart, so that the dead person could pass safely into the afterlife.

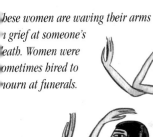

These women are waving their arms in grief at someone's death. Women were sometimes hired to mourn at funerals.

Ruling Egypt

The king of Egypt was an absolute ruler with total power over his people. It was his responsibility to see that the Egyptian world was well-balanced, successful and prosperous. The king was also chief priest, though he delegated this authority to others. At the same time he was the empire's military leader, defending its territory against enemies. Since most of the people were farmers, taxes were charged on farm produce to pay for the royal family, and the hierarchy of priests and officials, scribes and soldiers. The king had a range of officials to help him administer the empire, including a chief minister, or vizier. The king's principal wife also had a great deal of influence, and some queens even took the title of "king."

Part of a king list from a temple at Abydos. King lists showed the names and titles of rulers of Egypt in hieroglyphs, sometimes including the length and important events of each reign. They were used by kings to celebrate the cult of their royal ancestors.

This painting shows Ramesses II fighting the Hittites from his war chariot. The king is shown on a much larger scale than the other warriors, as was usual in Egyptian art.

The king was the chief priest of every religious cult, and in theory only he could make offerings to a god. This metal statue shows Tuthmosis IV (ruled 1419–1386 BC) offering two pots.

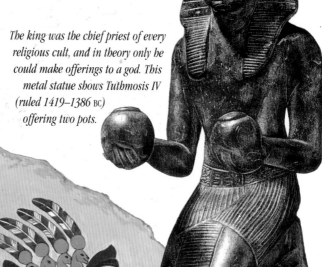

Egyptian queen

We call the king's wife "queen" but to the Egyptians she was the "great royal wife." Neferti (shown above in a painte limestone bust) was the principal wife of King Athenaten, and sh exerted great power over th empire. A few women actual ruled Egypt as pharaoh. Quee Hatshepsut (1473–1458 BC) too over when her husband died an her son was still very young. Sh had herself crowned "king," an some of her monuments show he in a king's costume and wearing royal bear

Foreign polic

The Egyptians believed that they were superior everyone else in the ancient world. Their greate rivals were the Hittites to the north (in presen day Turkey and Syria) and the Nubians to th south, who lived beyond Upper Egypt the higher reaches of the Nile. Nubi was rich in gold, and so th Egyptians were intereste in trade as well conquest. It was the king duty to keep his peopl safe, and this would hav been the main factor i shaping his attitude towar all foreigner

The symbols of kingship

This gold bust of Tutankhamun formed the head of one of his coffin lids. At the front of his nemes headcloth (1), the boy-king has images of Nekhbet (2), the vulture goddess of Upper Egypt, and Uto (3), the cobra goddess of Lower Egypt. As further symbols of kingship, Tutankhamun wears a braided false beard (4) and carries the royal crook (5) as a sign of government, and a flail (6), which was associated with the gods Osiris and Min and was probably originally a fly swatter or a grain-beater.

Tutankhamun's tomb

In 1922, an archaeologist named Howard Carter found the entrance to a small tomb in the Valley of the Kings. It was near the much larger tomb of Ramesses VI, and seemed quite insignificant. But when Carter went into the tomb, he found it full of what he called "wonderful things." Besides the gold coffins and mummy of the boy-king Tutankhamun, there were gilded couches, caskets, vases, parts of a chariot and many other beautiful objects. It was one of the greatest archaeological finds of the 20th century.

This picture of Tutankhamun and his queen is carved on the back of a golden throne. It shows Ankhesenamun anointing her husband with perfume.

Taxes were charged on farm produce, as well as numbers of livestock, from cattle to geese. This painting shows how taxes were calculated. They were normally paid in produce, and also sometimes in goods.

Counting crops

This wall painting from a tomb, dating from around 1400 BC, shows how agriculture was administered. When the grain was ripe, a land surveyor (1) used string knotted at regular intervals to measure the size of fields in cubits. Later, when the grain had been harvested, it was put into jars (2) and measured in hekats; 16 hekats made a khar, or sackful. The results are recorded by scribes (3). Menena (4), shown here in a pavilion supervising the survey, was a high official. The painting was found in his tomb.

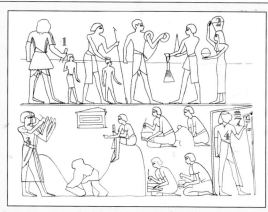

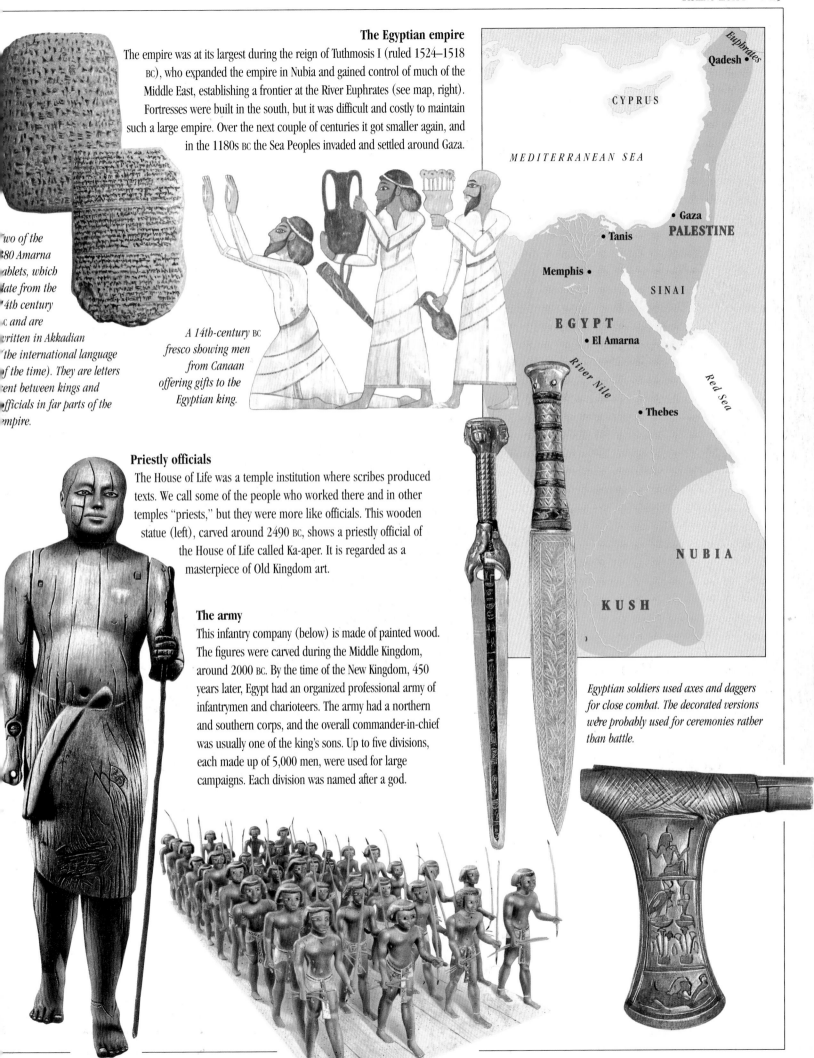

The Egyptian empire

The empire was at its largest during the reign of Tuthmosis I (ruled 1524–1518 BC), who expanded the empire in Nubia and gained control of much of the Middle East, establishing a frontier at the River Euphrates (see map, right). Fortresses were built in the south, but it was difficult and costly to maintain such a large empire. Over the next couple of centuries it got smaller again, and in the 1180s BC the Sea Peoples invaded and settled around Gaza.

Two of the 380 Amarna tablets, which date from the 14th century BC and are written in Akkadian (the international language of the time). They are letters sent between kings and officials in far parts of the empire.

A 14th-century BC fresco showing men from Canaan offering gifts to the Egyptian king.

Priestly officials

The House of Life was a temple institution where scribes produced texts. We call some of the people who worked there and in other temples "priests," but they were more like officials. This wooden statue (left), carved around 2490 BC, shows a priestly official of the House of Life called Ka-aper. It is regarded as a masterpiece of Old Kingdom art.

The army

This infantry company (below) is made of painted wood. The figures were carved during the Middle Kingdom, around 2000 BC. By the time of the New Kingdom, 450 years later, Egypt had an organized professional army of infantrymen and charioteers. The army had a northern and southern corps, and the overall commander-in-chief was usually one of the king's sons. Up to five divisions, each made up of 5,000 men, were used for large campaigns. Each division was named after a god.

Egyptian soldiers used axes and daggers for close combat. The decorated versions were probably used for ceremonies rather than battle.

Daily Life

Most ordinary Egyptian men worked on the land, producing enough to feed themselves and their families. They lived with their wife and children in houses made of sun-dried mud bricks. These were quite bare, with a few stools and low tables. Wealthier families had larger houses, with guest rooms and beautiful gardens. Most women married young and devoted themselves to their families. Women did all the work at home, with the help of servants if they could afford them. Some women did their own spinning, but most was done by professional weavers. Girls helped their mothers, while boys usually learned their father's trade. Skilled craftsmen such as carpenters were in great demand, and all towns and villages had workshops where everyday items were made.

The Egyptians enjoyed family life. Parents, especially mothers, spent as much time as they could with their children. Egyptian artists always painted children as much smaller than they really were, to show that they were not fully grown and perhaps not as important.

Children and young people, both boys and girls, usually had their heads shaved to leave a sidelock or tress that hung down over one ear. The sidelock was sometimes braided and decorated. Many adults had their hair completely shaved off, but those who had hair looked after it carefully. Wigs were common, especially for women.

Clothes

Egyptian clothes were made of white linen, which was woven from fibers of the flax plant (see the parents, above). People went to a great deal of trouble to make sure that their clothes were clean and neat. Because the climate was hot, workers often wore simple loincloths, and servant girls sometimes wore just a belt. Children often wore very little or nothing while they were playing (as in the picture above). Rich people wore the best linen for their tunics and kilts, but their style was still quite simple and it changed very little over thousands of years.

Most men worked in the fields, except during the season of the flood, and the work must have been hard. They used donkeys to carry harvested grain to storage granaries after it had been threshed. During busy farming periods, women sometimes took their husbands a cooked meal at midday so that they did not have to stop work.

Cooking

This wooden figure (right) shows a man fanning the fire to roast a duck. Meat was roasted or stewed in pots, and ox meat was the most highly valued but very expensive. Most food was cooked in clay ovens in the courtyard, to keep smoke and smells out of the house. Poorer people with just one room cooked over a fire made in a hole in the floor. Preparing food and cooking took up a lot of most women's time, but in larger households there were servants to do everyday jobs.

Basket-making was common, mainly using palm leaves. This was useful for household objects, such as this basket lid, stool and brush.

Many containers were made of pottery, and the potter's wheel was in use in Egypt before 2000 BC. Some pottery was imported, such as this beautiful vase from Mycenae.

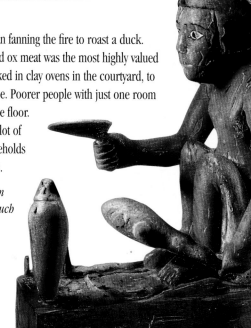

A carpenter's workshop

This painted wooden model was found in the private Theban tomb of Meketra. It dates from around 2000 BC. The model shows a group of carpenters hard at work, while others rest. The carpenter in the middle is using a long saw (1) to cut a plank of wood, which is tied to a post (2) to hold it firm; the saw was pulled through timber, rather than being pushed like a modern one. Three other carpenters are using adzes (3) to shape a plank. Another is using a wooden mallet (4) and chisel. Other tools (5), including axes and burins, are laid out on top of a storage chest, ready for use.

Main foods

The two main items of the Egyptian diet were bread and beer. Bread was made at home by housewives or servants, mainly from emmer wheat, and later villages had bakeries. Beer was made from barley, both at home and by professional brewers. It was a thick, nutritious brew, and it was not as alcoholic as it usually is today. Sometimes it was flavored with spices, honey and dates. At home, food was served in pottery dishes at low tables, and everyone ate with their fingers.

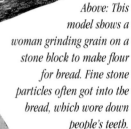

Above: This model shows a woman grinding grain on a stone block to make flour for bread. Fine stone particles often got into the bread, which wore down people's teeth.

One of the best Egyptian woods was sycamore fig, which was used to make coffins, tables and chests. Early metal tools were made of hardened copper. Later bronze was used, and some iron tools were probably imported.

Queens had plenty of time to enjoy their favorite pastimes. This painting shows Nefertari (c.1300–1250 BC), the principal wife of King Ramesses II, playing a game of senet. This board game was popular at all levels of Egyptian society.

A senet box, with a drawer for keeping the pieces. The game was for two players, who threw sticks or knucklebones to move their pieces around the board. Landing on certain squares meant moving forward or back, in a similar way to chutes and ladders.

Entertainment

The richer members of Egyptian society had plenty of time to amuse themselves, and they hired professional entertainers for banquets and other events. Ordinary people spent most of their time working, but they also managed to enjoy themselves. They all looked forward to the great public festivals, such as New Year (in July, when the flood started and the farmers had little work to do) and the Festival of the Potter's Wheel. Most other festivals were dedicated to gods. They were celebrated as public holidays, and for several days there was a lot of singing, dancing, eating and drinking. At home, boys and girls played simple running, jumping and catching games, and they also had toys and kept animals such as cats and monkeys as pets. There were games for adults, too, including a popular board game called senet.

Music and dance

Both music and dance, which went together, were performed by professionals for the entertainment of guests. Young girls did most of the dancing, and there are no records of men and women dancing together. For their music the Egyptians had string instruments, including harps, lutes and lyres, as well as wind and percussion instruments. They kept people entertained at public festivals. A special rattle, called a sistrum, was carried and played by noblewomen and priestesses at religious ceremonies.

Some women were professional musicians, providing entertainment for others. This woman is playing a lyre.

Dancers performed at special events. Female dancers were very acrobatic, specializing in somersaults, cartwheels and handstands.

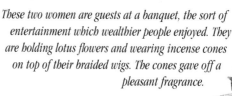

These two women are guests at a banquet, the sort of entertainment which wealthier people enjoyed. They are holding lotus flowers and wearing incense cones on top of their braided wigs. The cones gave off a pleasant fragrance.

This humorous ink drawing of an Egyptian legend shows a cat wielding a stick to drive a flock of geese. The Egyptians probably enjoyed telling stories and passed them from generation to generation.

Hunting and fishing

Hunting was a favorite pastime for the richer members of Egyptian society. In addition to fish and water birds, crocodiles and hippopotamuses were hunted in the marshes. Hunting parties for hippos were made up of many boats, and the animals were killed with spears. Lions and wild deer were hunted in the desert, and by the time of the New Kingdom the pharaoh himself took part in hunting big game such as lions, elephants and rhinoceroses. Fishing probably appealed more to the king's subjects, who would have found any catch a welcome addition to their diet.

Above: Fishermen using nets and traps to catch fish in the River Nile. Nets may sometimes have been dragged along the river between two boats. Young people especially probably saw boating and fishing as a sport.

Many water birds lived in the marshes around the Nile, and this was a popular form of hunting.

Below: Fish were sometimes harpooned, and catching fish with hooks on a line is also recorded. Certain fish were sacred in some areas and were therefore not caught.

Hunting in the marshes

This wall painting comes from a tomb chapel at Thebes and dates from around 1400 BC. It shows the scribe Nebamun (1) hunting for birds in the Nile marshes. He holds three live herons (2) in his right hand, to act as decoys, and is about to launch a throwstick (3) with his left. Nebamun's wife (4) is elaborately dressed, and their daughter (5) wears the sidelock of youth. The family's cat (6) has been brought on the trip, and is attacking some birds. The goose (7) at the prow of the boat may also have been a decoy. The marshes are full of papyrus reeds (8), and the river is teeming with fish (9).

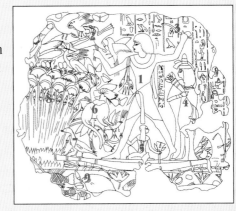

Paints and colors

Most painting in tombs and elsewhere was done on plastered surfaces. First the surface was divided into a grid of squares, onto which draftsmen drew an outline of the picture. Painters then colored in, before the draftsmen restored the outlines, usually in dark brown or black. Yellow, red and brown colors came from the mineral called ocher. White came from lime and was also mixed with other colors to lighten them. Blue was made by grinding a copper substance to powder, and black pigment was usually made from soot.

Coffin painting

This painting adorned the wooden coffin of Amenemopet, a priest of Amun, in his tomb in western Thebes. It dates from 950–900 BC. In the painting, Amenemopet (1) is dressed in a priest's leopard-skin robe (2) on top of his linen tunic. He is making an offering to Osiris (3), the god of the underworld who was identified with kings when they died (see page 15). Osiris is holding the flail (4) with which he was associated and which became one of the symbols of Egyptian kingship. On top of the offering table (5) are two lotus flowers (6) which served as the emblem of Upper Egypt.

Art

ost of the earliest pieces of Egyptian art that survived for later archaeologists to study were carved in stone. One of the earliest royal sculptures is an almost life-size seated statue of King Djoser, from around 2650 BC. Relief sculpture, or wall carving, decorated the walls of temples and tombs in the Old Kingdom. Scenes were carved in rows, and people are shown in profile. Much less painting has survived from earlier periods, not surprisingly, but it had a similar design to the carvings. Outlines were drawn first, and then filled in with even, flat colors. The New Kingdom period from 1570 to 1070 BC produced so many brilliant paintings in Theban tombs that it is sometimes called the "golden age" of Egyptian painting. Though overall styles did not change dramatically over thousands of years, individual techniques improved and became more complex.

Part of an ornamental pectoral, or breastplate, from the Ptolemaic period (332–30 BC). It is made of glass paste encrusted with gold and silver. The art of glassmaking was probably first introduced into Egypt in the 15th century BC, and the Egyptians seem to have regarded glass almost as a precious stone.

Tutankhamun's throne is made of sheets of gold, inlaid with colored glass and semiprecious stones, on top of a wooden frame. The legs have lions' heads at the top and lions' legs and feet below.

Jewelry

From very early times the Egyptians used gold, lapis lazuli, turquoise and amethyst in items of jewelry. By the time of the Middle Kingdom, jewelers were producing works of great elegance, much of which has survived because it was buried with the owners in tombs. Craftsmen used tools called bow-drills to pierce beads and other jewels, and they inlaid jewels into wood, metal and glass paste. Poorer people also wore simple jewelry.

One of more than 200 pieces of jewelry found in Tutankhamun's tomb. It is made of gold, with inset semiprecious stones. The wedjat eye at the top represents the eye of Horus and was put there to ward off evil.

This ceramic vessel was turned on a potter's wheel. Its tall, long-necked shape and style of painting are typical of the New Kingdom period, when pottery became more decorative. It also has the "wedjat eye" painted on it. After this period, pots went back to being more useful, everyday items.

Gold

There were many gold mines between the River Nile and the Red Sea, and the Egyptians loved this precious metal. Gold was beaten into shape or molten and cast in molds. Goldsmiths also used a method called granulation, by which granules of gold were stuck to an object by soldering. Thin sheets of gold were easy to work, and were used to cover wooden statues and other objects (such as the figure and the throne, left). Gold was regarded as a divine metal and associated with the gods, especially Ra.

Figure in gilded wood of the goddess Serket, who was one of four goddesses who protected Tutankhamun's coffin and canopic jars (containing the internal organs). On top of her head is a rearing scorpion, since she was regarded as the scorpion goddess.

This bronze vessel, called a situla, was used to hold water taken from a sacred lake next to a temple. It was used by priests to sprinkle holy water during special ceremonies, and the base was tapered to allow it to rest on a stand. Bronze was also used, as copper had been earlier, to make household pots and utensils, as well as tools and weapons.

Science and Trade

This gold coin was minted around 350 BC, probably in Memphis. The hieroglyphic inscription on the front (top) reads "fine gold."

Foreign slaves became more common in Egypt when the empire expanded and trade increased. Most slaves were prisoners of war. Some were owned by communities rather than individuals, and they may have helped to increase the production of goods for further trade.

The Egyptians used their science and technology for practical purposes, such as predicting the Nile flood, and constructing amazing temples, pyramids and other tombs. It seems that they did not create general laws based on the practical solutions they found, unlike the later ancient Greeks, but experts have varying views on the Egyptians' knowledge and use of astronomy and mathematics. Some believe that the pyramids were used as astronomical observatories. The Egyptians certainly developed accurate systems of measurement, which were used for trade and taxation purposes, since the first coins were only introduced during the 29th dynasty (399–380 BC). Foreign trade was mainly done by barter (exchanging goods of equal value), and trading expeditions were regularly sent to the Mediterranean regions and beyond. Gold, papyrus, linen and grain were Egypt's main exports, and imports included heavy, strong wood, spices, gemstones and later iron. Diplomatic gifts were also exchanged with other nations, which was a good way of obtaining luxury goods for those at the top of Egyptian society.

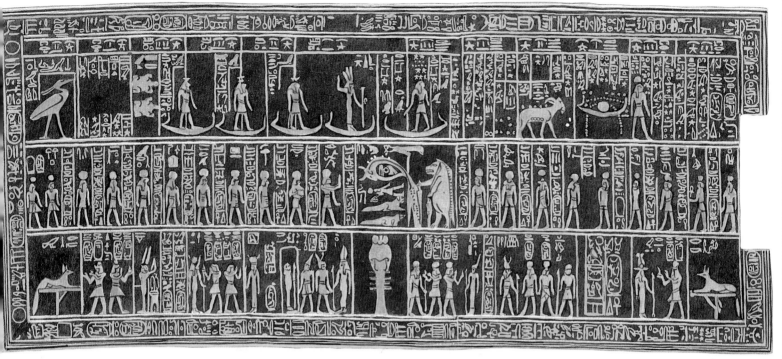

his hieroglyphic calendar shows the year divided into three seasons (see page 8). he year began on the first day that Sirius, the dog star, reappeared after 70 days during which it was eclipsed by the sun. This was exactly when the annual flood was expected to begin and corresponds to our date of July 19. The Egyptians were clearly keen astronomical observers, and we know that they recognized five of the planets as early as the Middle Kingdom. They based their month on the cycle of the moon.

Heavenly constellations

The ceiling of the burial chamber of King Seti I (1294–1279 BC), in the Valley of the Kings, is beautifully decorated in black and yellow paint. The painting includes the twelve hours of the night (1), and various star constellations: Orion (2), represented by the god Sah, who was known as the "glorious soul of Osiris;" Sirius (3), the "dog star," represented by the goddess Sopdet, the wife of Sah; and Taurus (4), as the constellation was later known. The "astronomical ceiling" was painted to appear directly above the coffin containing the mummy of the dead king. Perhaps the intention was that Seti's soul could ascend directly into the sky above.

Metal weights, such as this one in the shape of a rabbit, were made in units known as debens. They were used to describe the value of goods.

This alabaster container was used to measure liquids and dates from New Kingdom times (1570–1070 BC). The stone weights were used in the same way as metal weights; lighter ones were made of pottery.

Measuring things

A knowledge of weights and measures was important to Egyptian trade, as well as to science. Since there were no coins until later times, weights were used to express the value of things, using the basic unit of a deben. We know from some lists of property that a goat was valued at 1 deben, while a bed was worth 2.5 deben, but these values probably fluctuated. As the basic unit of measurement, the royal cubit was measured by rods (see below) or knotted string (see page 24). The volume of liquids and materials such as grain was measured in containers.

A gilded wooden cubit-rod from about 1370 BC. The royal cubit (around 21 inches), based on the length of a man's forearm, was the main unit of measurement.

An official uses weights on a pair of scales to weigh gold rings in the royal treasury. The results were then recorded on papyrus rolls. These records helped show the value of things, which was essential for successful trading.

Writing and Literature

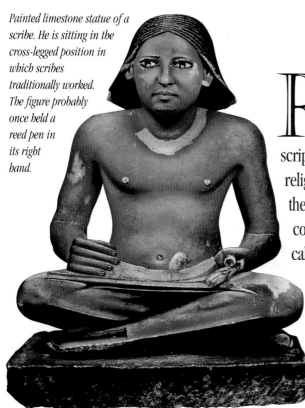

Painted limestone statue of a scribe. He is sitting in the cross-legged position in which scribes traditionally worked. The figure probably once held a reed pen in its right hand.

R ecent discoveries have shown that the Egyptians were already using the ancient script that we call hieroglyphics by about 3250 BC. The word hieroglyph comes from the Greek for "sacred carving", and we call the script that because it was mainly used to write inscriptions on temples, tombs and religious documents. More than 6,000 hieroglyphic signs have been identified, but the script was used and understood by very few ancient Egyptians. Most people could not read or write. From early dynastic times scribes used an easier script called hieratic for everyday writing, and this was later replaced by an even speedier script called demotic. Spells and texts to help dead people on their journey to the afterlife were written in pyramids, and these later developed into papyrus rolls that we call the Book of the Dead. They were written in all three Egyptian scripts, and most rich people had them placed in their coffin.

The scribe

Scribes were important and highly thought of. Their work was seen as the opposite of manual labor, which was what occupied most Egyptians. The hieroglyphic sign for "writing" (left) shows a reed brush attached to a red water-bag, which scribes used to make ink from black and red cakes of pigment.

The papyrus plant was used to make writing material. Squares of papyrus were fixed together into a roll. This one has been written on in the hieratic script.

These hieroglyphs were beautifully carved and painted on a wooden coffin lid in the 4th century BC, and show a high level of craftsmanship. The owl stood for the letter "m."

This scarab charm tells of important events in the life of King Amenhotep III. Scarabs were made in the shape of sacred dung beetles.

Jean-François Champollion (1790–1832), a French linguist and Egyptologist, deciphered hieroglyphics from the Rosetta Stone (right).

The Rosetta Stone is inscribed with hieroglyphics (top), demotic (center) and Greek (bottom). The stone is just over 3 feet tall.

This seal bears the name and title of an army officer. The plumed horse in the left-hand column stands for "cavalry," and the bull on the right represents the officer's name (Ka-nakht, or "strong bull").

The Rosetta Stone

In 1822 Jean-François Champollion used this carved slab to decipher ancient Egyptian scripts. This was made possible by the fact that the same text was written in three different scripts. The text itself dates from 196 BC and is a record of benefits conferred on Egypt by Ptolemy V. The content was not really important to historians, but the ability to read hieroglyphics gave them – and us – great insight into the ancient Egyptian world.

scribe at work. Scribes used
*red brushes to write on chips
of stone, fragments of pottery,
leather sheets and wooden boards, as
well as on papyrus.*

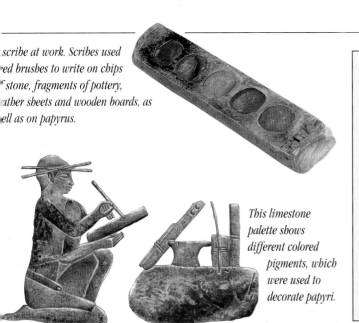

*This limestone
palette shows
different colored
pigments, which
were used to
decorate papyri.*

Temple of Tuthmosis III

Hieroglyphs adorn the rear wall of the
temple, which shows Tuthmosis III
(1504–1450 BC) (1) offering water and
incense to Amun-Ra (2). The delicate
feathers on his crown (3) show him to
be the highest god of the New Kingdom.
The two cartouches show two of the
king's names; the birth name (4) is
headed "Son of Ra" (5), and the
coronation name (6) is headed "He of
the sedge and the bee" (7), which meant "King of Upper and Lower Egypt." The right-
hand column (8) reads, "Amun-Ra, lord of the two lands, god of the sky", who says to
the king, "I give you life, power, stability and joy, as the eternal Ra."

Index

The publishers would like to thank the following picture libraries and photographers for permission to reproduce their photos:

Cover: *Tomb of Pharaoh Horemheb*, The Valley of the Kings (Frank Teichmann, Stuttgart)

7, 8-9 Jürgen Liepe, Berlin; 11 Corbis/Grazia Neri; 14-15 Frank Teichmann, Stuttgart; 19 White Star; 20 Abdel Ghaffar Shedid, Munich; 23 Jürgen Liepe, Berlin; 24 Lotos Film, Kaufbeuren; 27 Jürgen Liepe, Berlin; 30 British Museum; 32 Abdel Ghaffar Shedid, Munich; 35 Jürgen Liepe, Berlin.